DISNEP
Aladdin

SONGS FROM THE MOTION PICTURE SOUNDTRACK

ISBN 978-1-5400-5996-3

HAL•LEONARD®

Visit Hal Leonard Online at
www.halleonard.com

Contact us:
Hal Leonard
7777 West Bluemound Road
Milwaukee, WI 53213
Email: info@halleonard.com

In Europe, contact:
Hal Leonard Europe Limited
42 Wigmore Street
Marylebone, London, W1U 2RN
Email: info@halleonardeurope.com

In Australia, contact:
Hal Leonard Australia Pty. Ltd.
4 Lentara Court
Cheltenham, Victoria, 3192 Australia
Email: info@halleonard.com.au

Contents

ARABIAN NIGHTS
(2019)

Music by ALAN MENKEN
Lyrics by HOWARD ASHMAN,
BENJ PASEK and JUSTIN PAUL

Oh, im-ag-ine a land,__ it's a far-a-way place__ where the
car-a-van cam-els roam, where you wan-der a-mong__ ev-'ry
cul-ture and tongue.__ It's cha-ot-ic, but hey, it's home. When the

ONE JUMP AHEAD

Music by ALAN MENKEN
Lyrics by TIM RICE

Very bright two

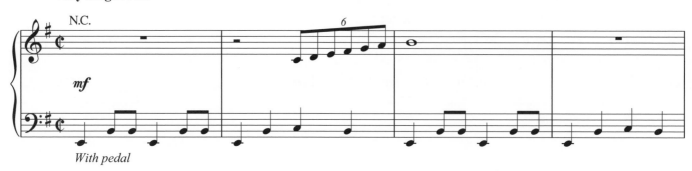

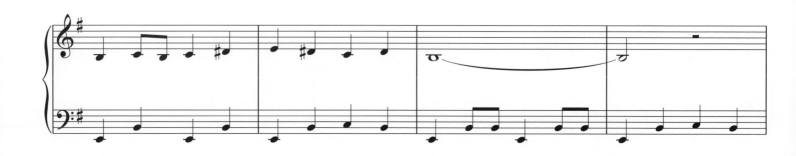

ONE JUMP AHEAD
(Reprise)

Music by ALAN MENKEN
Lyrics by TIM RICE

FRIEND LIKE ME

Music by ALAN MENKEN
Lyrics by HOWARD ASHMAN

Bright Big Band Shuffle

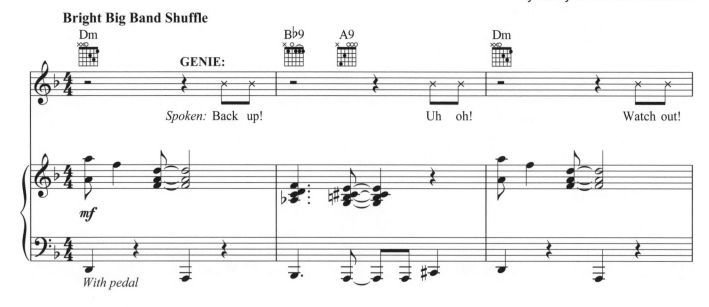

GENIE:

Spoken: Back up! Uh oh! Watch out!

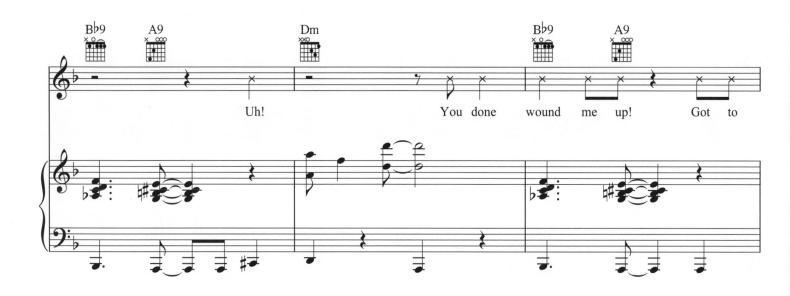

Uh! You done wound me up! Got to

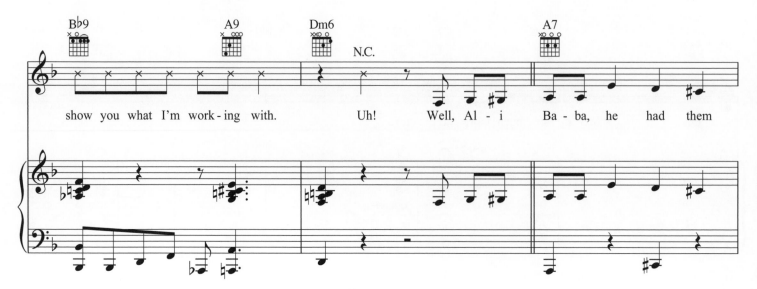

show you what I'm work-ing with. Uh! Well, Al-i Ba-ba, he had them

34

PRINCE ALI

Music by ALAN MENKEN
Lyrics by HOWARD ASHMAN

A WHOLE NEW WORLD

Music by ALAN MENKEN
Lyrics by TIM RICE

ALADDIN:
I can show you the world, shin - ing, shim-mer-ing, splen - did.

Tell me, Prin - cess, now when did you last let your heart de - cide? ___

ONE JUMP AHEAD
(Reprise 2)

Music by ALAN MENKEN
Lyrics by TIM RICE

SPEECHLESS

Music by ALAN MENKEN
Lyrics by BENJ PASEK
and JUSTIN PAUL

Here comes a wave __ meant to wash __ me a-way, __ a tide that is tak-ing me un-der. __ Swal-low-ing sand, __ left with noth - ing to say, __ my voice drowned out __ in the thun - der. __ But I won't